Chicago

Text by Marilyn D. Clancy
Photography by Ron Schramm

Voyageur Press

This book was developed by the Goddard Book Group, Chicago.
Connie Goddard, Principal.

Edited by Todd R. Berger
Designed by Kathryn Mallien and Andrea Rud
Printed in Hong Kong

96 97 98 99 5 4 3 2

Library of Congress Cataloging-in-Publication Data
Clancy, Marilyn D.
Chicago / text by Marilyn D. Clancy ; photography by Ron Schramm.
    p.   cm.
Includes bibliographical references (p. 94) and index.
ISBN 0-89658-318-X
1. Chicago (Ill.)—Pictorial works. 2. Chicago (Ill.)—Description and travel.
I. Schramm, Ron.
F548.37.C58 1995
977.3'11—dc20   95-20329
                                                                  CIP

Distributed in Canada by Raincoast Books, 8680 Cambie Street,
Vancouver, B.C. V6P 6M9

Published by Voyageur Press, Inc.
123 North Second Street, P.O. Box 338, Stillwater, MN 55082 U.S.A.
612-430-2210, fax 612-430-2211

Please write or call, or stop by, for our free catalog of natural history publications.
Our toll-free number to place an order or to obtain a free catalog is
800-888-WOLF (800-888-9653).

*Educators, fundraisers, premium and gift buyers, publicists, and marketing
managers:* Looking for creative products and new sales ideas? Voyageur Press
books are available at special discounts when purchased in quantities, and
special editions can be created to your specifications. For details contact our
marketing department.

*Page 1: Approaching downtown Chicago via South Lake Shore Drive offers an awe-inspir-
ing sight of this modern metropolis. Parklands border both sides of the drive, yielding an
unobstructed view of the city's skyscrapers.*

Acknowledgments

I would like to thank Connie Goddard for bringing us together to do this delightful project. We all learned a lot about the city and became better friends along the way. I would also like to thank Jean Hunt, who knows more about Chicago history than anyone and shares her knowledge with enthusiasm. And finally, I would like to express my gratitude to Dorothy Coyle of the Chicago Office of Tourism, who patiently answered every question she could.
D.C.

I thank the people of Chicago. Their help along the way was instrumental in taking these photographs. During our conversations while I made photographs or accessed a certain vantage point of the city, Chicagoans were always friendly and helpful.
R.S.

Dedication

To Bill Clancy, who has taught me a lot about Chicago and life—always with a joyful heart and passionate spirit. And to our four children—Michelle, Michael, Colette, and Timothy—whose curiosity and gusto expanded our world and made it so much more fun.
D.C.

To my wife, Ann.
R.S.

This young visitor to the Lincoln Park Conservatory enjoys one of the ever-changing flower shows. More than one million visitors view the impressive collections of exotic plants and trees here and at the Garfield Park Conservatory on the west side.

Contents

Left: *A white picket fence borders part of Lincoln Park's Farm in the Zoo and offers a rural accent to the bustling urban residential area beyond.*

Opposite: *Chicago Place, another upscale vertical mall along North Michigan Avenue, incorporates several Prairie-style motifs into its design. In the 1960s, a visionary developer annointed this once-restrained promenade the Magnificent Mile, and to the dismay of some traditionalists, his vision has been largely realized since then.*

Introduction

As I grew up on the north side, in an area known as Uptown, my Chicago was only as broad as my experiences in the neighborhood. After I went away to boarding school fifty miles from Chicago, my city expanded as I visited my school chums in Little Italy and Hyde Park and South Chicago. But I didn't yet know that Chicago had seventy-seven distinct neighborhoods. To me, this huge metropolis seemed more like a series of little fiefdoms, each with its own main street—Taylor Street, Midway Plaisance, Blue Island and Milwaukee Avenues. My border crossings were by bus, subway, electric train, and the "El" (as Chicagoans call the elevated train). Occasionally, my dad would take me for a Sunday drive in the car, but every other day getting around town was strictly by public transportation.

Back then I didn't know that elevated trains were invented here in 1892 to carry fair-goers to the 1893 World's Columbian Exposition in Jackson Park on the city's south side. I was only aware of my excitement, tinged with fear, as the El screeched into the subway tunnel south of the Fullerton stop. I pretended to be a spy headed downtown on some mysterious mission. Since then, I've taken variations of that El/subway ride thousands of times, and I consider it a miracle that I'm not deaf, given the steel-on-steel racket of the Chicago Transit Authority (CTA) trains careening around curves and screaming into the stations. As an adult, I've used other subway systems in San Francisco; Washington, DC; Paris; and Mexico City, but something was wrong. They were so quiet. I felt like I was in a dream sequence sans the sound and fury and the reality of my simultaneously beloved and hated CTA.

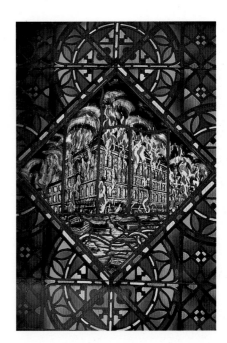

Above: A stained-glass window along the east wall of the Chicago Temple at Clark and Washington commemorates the Great Chicago Fire of 1871.

Opposite: Paddleboats at rest in Lincoln Park's South Pond provide a peaceful frontispiece for the thriving and elegant area known as the Gold Coast.

View of Streeterville from North Avenue.

I have my own special memories of Lake Michigan as well. Montrose Beach was my childhood playground, on a lake I thought was an ocean, with a horizon that fell off the edge of the earth. Later I learned that Lake Michigan is one of the largest freshwater lakes in the world. In my youth, I only knew it was beautiful and always cold, and that one day my stepmother, aunt, and I caught sixty-eight perch in it! On one August night, our family and hundreds of others slept overnight in the park near Montrose Beach (that was before "Park closes at 11 P.M." signs were posted all over). We all were trying to escape the warm, stagnant air of our un–air-conditioned apartments; a week of 90- and 100-degree temperatures had made home intolerable. The parks of Chicago likely improved the morale of a good portion of the city's population as they went to work the next day.

At the time, I knew that this park and beach of mine merged with others to the north and south. By chance, I had learned that you could walk through lakefront parks all the way from downtown to my neighborhood, a delightful discovery made when I lost my carfare home. Today, I know that Chicago has twenty-nine miles of public lakefront shoreline. According to an 1836 document plotting the city, our lakefront is to remain "forever open, clear and free of any buildings, or other obstruction whatsoever." We have Aaron Montgomery Ward to thank especially for holding the city fathers and developers to that early promise. Between 1890 and 1911, Ward sued the city four times to keep it "from filling the park with public buildings." Ward took time away from his ledgers to save the green space that is the front-yard playground of the city today.

Montgomery Ward's, as I saw it as a child, was simply a huge mail-order house selling everything from garden rakes to underpants. Later I found out that mail order shopping was born in Chicago. Ward's and Sears and Speigel and Marshall Field's and a host of other smaller stores revolutionized American shopping.

But shopping convenience aside, you can't grow up in Chicago and not love sports. My friends and I were "bleacher bums" at Wrigley Field. However, when I went to watch Cubs games with my dad, we sat in box seats. Then, as now, Chicagoans defined themselves by whether they were Cubs or Sox fans and ne'er the twain would meet. Today "da three Bs"—Bears, Blackhawks, and Bulls—seem to enjoy universal support. Is there another American city with such a plethora of teams and sports fever? I think not! And where else do they play with such abandon a game called 16-inch softball,

a gloveless version of the original requiring only a bat and a ball?

As a child visiting my father's office, ten miles and two long bus rides away on the northwest side, I passed what at first I thought was a country estate with a lawn that appeared to have been trimmed with fingernail scissors. That was (and still is) the headquarters of M & M/Mars, the candy company that makes Milky Ways, Mars Bars, Snickers, and Three Musketeers. Chicago is the candy capital of the world: Red Hots, Boston Baked Beans, Gummi Bears and Worms, Atomic Fireballs, Lemon Heads, Tootsie Rolls, and Fannie Mays roll off tasty assembly lines daily. Cracker Jack was invented here and first distributed at the 1893 Columbian Exposition, though the prizes were not added until 1912, and the biggest cookie and cracker factory in the world, Nabisco, making around 2.4 billion Oreos per year (!), is on the southwest side. When the wind is right, natives and visitors alike salivate over the chocolate aroma that wafts across the river from the Blommer's factory just west of the city center. Sweet home Chicago indeed!

My west-side Irish husband (and that's west-side as distinct from south-side Irish) says his family's fortunes were reflected by which streetcar line they lived on. They moved to the more affluent west in good

times and retreated to the east when times were tough. But regardless of his family's material wealth, there were always streetcar lines a short distance away. The streetcars, following the principal thoroughfares to the farthest reaches of Chicago, connected the disparate neighborhoods of the city; now bus routes and the El do that.

Those same thoroughfares weave a perfectly gridlike pattern through Chicago's neighborhoods. In fact, it is almost impossible to get lost in the city. The numbering system begins downtown at State and Madison and marches north, south, and west (with a little dollop of east as the shoreline heads over to Indiana), following those evenly spaced arteries. We have a few diagonal streets, as well, which are vestiges of old Native American trails, and help Chicagoans get around town faster. Some portions of streets have honorary second names. So don't be surprised to see Mies van der Rohe on part of Seneca, Gandhi Marg and Golda Meir on Devon, Siskel and Ebert on Erie, Lou Rawls on 43rd, and Irv Kupcinet on the Wabash Avenue Bridge.

And, ah, the bridges of Cook County! They're not covered, but they move. In fact, Chicago has more movable bridges than any other city in the world—a total of fifty-two. The most illustrious, the Michigan Avenue Bridge, is a double-decked, double-leaf trunnion bascule (a mouthful, I know; just think "seesaw"). It stands a few steps from the site where Chicago's first permanent settler Jean Baptiste Point du Sable built his cabin in 1789 and where, in 1803, the U.S. Army established Fort Dearborn, as the country's frontier expanded westward. Today the bridge links Chicago's commercial center with the Magnificent Mile, the city's flower-filled *Champs Elysées*. The bridge spans the Chicago River, the only river in the world that flows backwards, (courtesy of Chicago's turn-of-the-century problem-solving genius) and the first, if not the only one, to be dyed green every St. Patrick's Day, a custom coinciding with the annual St. Patrick's Day Parade in March.

The Chicago panoply of parades begins with the Chinese New Year's Day Parade in January or February, followed by the St. Patrick's Day parade; the Greek-American and Polish Constitution Day parades in May; the Philippine Independence Day and Puerto Rican Day parades in June; the Bud Billiken Day and India Independence Day parades in August; the Mexican Independence Day and Von Steuben Day parades in September; and the Columbus Day Parade in October, to name a few. Hundreds of others march through Chicago's neighborhoods annually. The rich tapestry that is ethnic Chicago, one of the most racially and ethnically diverse cities in the country, is reflected in such neighborhood festivals. Native Americans, Japanese, Koreans, Swedes, Vietnamese, Ukrainians, African Americans, and others know what it means to celebrate. In addition, immigrants arrive daily, making the mosaic that is Chicago even more complex, colorful, and alive.

Over the years, I've read various descriptions of Chicago from travelers arriving from near and far. Their comments often portray the city in terms of grit and grime, a descent from the pristine prairie into an urban maelstrom. But that's not my Chicago. As an eight-year-old, I headed into the city center alone high atop an open-air double decker bus traveling along the breathtaking lakefront. I have also read about the belching smokestacks of the steel industry's blast furnaces and the stockyards, repugnant with strange smells and noises. Both are gone today because Chicago keeps reinventing itself. Yesterday's Hog Butcher to the World is today's futures and options exchange leader. Sometimes, it seems, a reputation changes a lot slower than reality.

People who don't live here have no idea of how incredibly bold and extraordinarily beautiful this city is. Edith Wharton's description of a summer afternoon as "the two most beautiful words in the English language" can be fully appreciated during a stroll through Lincoln Park or a picnic in Grant Park. The music of the parks's free festivals and concerts mesmerizes the summertime crowds, particularly the sounds of the Grant Park Concerts, the nation's oldest free outdoor concert series. The gentle breezes of Lake Michigan flow through the parks, with the sounds of the city center only a few steps away. "Chicago—The World's Biggest Surprise" shouted one international advertising campaign. What an understatement!

When I served as the director of the Chicago Tourism Council, I traveled around the United States and abroad promoting Chicago. The negative or, worse yet, nonexistent images people held about my city astonished me. They knew about gangster Al Capone, but not about Nobel Prize–winning University of Chicago physicist Albert Michaelson, whose institution boasts more Nobel Laureates—sixty-four—than any other institution in the world. They had heard of the Great

Chicago Fire of 1871, but they did not know that the entire city was virtually destroyed and then rebuilt as the architectural Athens of the New World. They knew Chicago had tall buildings, but had no idea that the modern skyscraper was invented here. They may have been aware of Chicago as a robust business city with one of the largest convention centers in the world, but they didn't know that the Chicago Symphony Orchestra is widely heralded as one of the best anywhere. They were completely in the dark about our Lyric Opera, which attracts a larger audience than any other opera company in the world, and about the Art Institute of Chicago, where so many of their favorite paintings are displayed.

Recently, however, the world's impression of Chicago has become closer to the reality of the city, an evolution connected with the dramatic arts. The 240 movies filmed in Chicago in the last few years—*Richy Rich, The Fugitive, About Last Night, When Harry Met Sally, The Untouchables, Ferris Bueller's Day Off, The Blues Brothers,* among others—have projected the city's incredible diversity and startling beauty on movie screens throughout the world. Playwrights David Mamet and the late Lorraine Hansberry have electrified audiences with their pure Chicago stories, *Glengarry Glen Ross* and *Raisin in the Sun.* In addition, Steppenwolf Theatre Ensemble members John Malkovich, Laurie Metcalf, William Petersen, Gary Cole, Gary Sinise, John Mahoney, and others have epitomized made-in-Chicago theatre as a training ground for greatness. Improvisational theatre also began here with the Compass Players at the University of Chicago. The original Compass Players included Elaine May, Mike Nichols, Shelley Berman, Alan Arkin, Jerry Stiller, and Ann Meara, and the group eventually evolved into Second City. A list of former members of that troupe reads like a who's who of contemporary talent: Dan Ackroyd, Alan Alda, Jane Alexander, Jim and John Belushi, John Candy, Barbara Harris, Shelley Long, Michael Meyers, Bill Murray, Gilda Radner, Joan Rivers, Valerie Harper, and on and on. In all, 150 theatre companies perform here on any given night.

High drama in Chicago also includes a certain political feistiness. In the 1890s, newspaper columnist Finley Peter Dunne introduced America to Chicago's official and unofficial shenanigans through his Irish alter-ego, Martin Dooley. Today Mike Royko carries on that tradition with his fictional Polish commentator, Slats Grobnik.

Chicago does indeed possess a rich political history. Chicago's first mayor, William B. Ogden, was a carpet-bagger who came from New York intent on unloading what he considered his family's risky land investments in Chicago. To his amazement and delight, the first parcel he sold, only one-third of his holdings, returned as much money as the entire original investment. He stayed in Chicago, and his legacy remains through the Chicago Dock and Canal Trust, the company he founded (which is still very active in Chicago development and owns a large hunk of chic Streeterville today) and Ogden Avenue, a diagonal thoroughfare that traverses the city. A few decades later, Abraham Lincoln was nominated for the Presidency of the United States in Chicago at the Republican Convention of 1860. Chicago has been host to more Presidential nominating conventions than any other American city, a fact little noted by those who only recall the 1968 debacle, which, incidentally, took place near an imposing statue of Lincoln in Grant Park.

But despite sometime controversy, Chicago is rightly recognized as a can-do town, characterized by the "I Will" figure created in 1891 to embody the spirit of Chicago. The city's imagination is overshadowed only by the chutzpah of its inventiveness. Roller skates were invented here in 1884; the Ferris wheel in 1893; the steel frame skyscraper in 1895; the zipper in 1896; the window envelope in 1902; pinball in 1930; and the first nuclear chain reaction in 1942. It appears that Chicago invented the modern world.

In the Old World, all roads led to Rome. In the new one, all airways, super highways, railroad lines, and waterways lead to (or through) Chicago. One hundred and fifty years ago, Chicagoans figured out how to link the Great Lakes with the Gulf of Mexico by building the Illinois and Michigan Canal. One hundred years ago they brought twenty-six million people here to visit the World's Columbian Exposition of 1893. In 1933 and 1934, forty million visitors came to Chicago's Century of Progress Exposition. In 1994, two billion people viewed the opening ceremonies of the World Cup competition held at Soldier Field, albeit most through the electronic marvel of satellite TV. Each year, four million business people—a number that exceeds the city's population—come for meetings, conventions, and trade shows; another twenty-two million leisure visitors arrive to sample pleasures that are to be found only in Chicago. In all, sixty-six million travelers used Chicago's O'Hare International Airport in 1994, making it the world's busiest.

It's difficult to decide which of the city's wonders attracts the largest number of visitors or gives Chicagoans the greatest reason to strut. Is it the museum-like quality and range of its architecture? Or is it the Picasso in the Daley Center Plaza, which asks the curious to decide whether it is a lady or a bird? Maybe it is the outdoor sculptures of Chagall, Calder, Miro, Dubuffet, Moore, or Nevelson? Or the 150 museums in the area? Perhaps the rhythms of the city have drawn (or kept) them here—from the swing of Benny Goodman and the gospel of Mahalia Jackson and Thomas A. Dorsey, to the rock of Liz Phair and the salsa of the neighborhoods, not to mention the free, world-class blues, gospel, country music, and jazz festivals on the lakefront each summer.

Then again, the lure of the city might be some of the other Chicago superlatives: three of the tallest buildings in the world; the world's largest indoor marine mammal pavilion; the world's largest public library; an endless lakefront on which to stroll, swim, bike, or rollerblade; one of the last free major zoos in the world; the spectacularly delicious Chicago-style deep-dish pan pizza or distinctive hot dogs; more professional sports teams than any other city in the country; the busiest futures exchange on the planet. Whatever it is, Chicago has it.

Chicago—city on the make, city of broad shoulders, the city that works, gem of the prairie, city with clout, the world on the lake, city of commerce, city of culture, city of neighborhoods, that toddlin' town, windy city, crossroads of a nation, Paris on the prairie—all are facets of the same complex treasure. Each aspect of Chicago has to be experienced to be understood. Our wish for your journey through Chicago—whether from your armchair with this book or atop a double-decker bus—is that you will have the opportunity to savor all of the wonders that are to be found only in Chicago.

City on the Water

In four score years, Chicago grew from an unpromising mudflat to the nation's second largest city, mainly due to its location. Here, the Great Lakes met the Mississippi River system, linking America's two great waterways via a brief portage between the Chicago River and the Des Plaines, which flows into the Illinois River and eventually the Mississippi. A spot known to Native Americans for centuries, the area was called *Checagou*, variously translated as wild onion, smelly garlic, or skunk grass.

Above: At Cermak Road, this rolling lift bridge crosses the South Branch of the Chicago River. Once at the center of the city's flourishing lumber business, this point on the river now serves primarily as a winter mooring spot for pleasure boats.

Opposite: The Sears Tower, completed in 1974 and still the world's tallest building, dominates Chicago's skyline from any angle. Here it's seen from Wolf Point (to the left, under the bridge), at the confluence of the North and South Branches of the Chicago River, a mile west of Lake Michigan.

Above: Flags of all nations flew from the Michigan Avenue Bridge during the summer of 1994, when Chicago was a host city for World Cup Soccer. Built in 1920, the double-decker bridge links the city's original commercial district known as the Loop with the North Michigan Avenue area, now called the Magnificent Mile and offering unrivaled opportunities for shopping and strolling. Tour boats leave from the west side of the bridge, in the shadow of the Wrigley Building (upper left), near where fur trader Jean Baptiste Point du Sable established Chicago's first commercial trading post in 1779.

Right: A bas relief called "The Pioneers" adorns one of the pylons on the Michigan Avenue Bridge. It commemorates settlers who followed du Sable, heading first for the security of Fort Dearborn, built in 1803 at a site just south of the bridge.

Left: Chicago boasts fifty-two movable bridges across its river, more than any other city in the world. Many of them are engineering marvels (a forty-horsepower engine begins the lifting action of the trunnion bascule bridges over the river's main branch downtown; after that, counterweights take over). The bridges were honored in this detail from the now demolished Ogden Avenue Bridge over the North Branch; this ornament will become part of the Art Institute's Fragments of Chicago's Past collection.

"'Chicago, the world on the lake'" has always been my favorite description of the city. The phrase captures the global-village quality of our city. Every culture, every cuisine can be found only in Chicago."
—Pat Matsumoto, cultural affairs official

The Kinzie Street Bridge, just north of Wolf Point, is one of the city's oldest bridges. It is also known as the origin of the Great Chicago Flood of 1992, apparently caused when pilings protecting the bridge ruptured Chicago's nearly forgotten underground tunnel system.

Once a warehouse, North Pier is now a trendy dining, shopping, entertainment, and office complex. It is located just north of the river's mouth on Ogden Slip, named for Chicago's first mayor.

"[Chicago is] a city wherein warmth of heart and a freezing greed beat, like the blood and the breath, as one. . . . Yet once you've come to be part of this particular patch, you'll never love another. Like loving a woman with a broken nose, you may well find lovelier lovelies. But never a lovely so real."
—Nelson Algren, from *Chicago: City on the Make*, 1951

Above: An excursion boat glides past Navy Pier on Lake Michigan. Built in 1916 as the Municipal Pier, it extends a half mile out into the lake. A Navy training facility during World War II and later the University of Illinois' Chicago campus, today it is an entertainment and convention center. The four stars on the Chicago flag (far right) recall four seminal events in the history of the city: the Fort Dearborn Massacre in 1812, the Great Chicago Fire in 1871, the World's Columbian Exposition in 1893, and the Century of Progress Exposition in 1933. The two bars of blue represent the two branches of the Chicago River, and the white spaces represent the northern, western, and southern sections of the city.

Right: Fireworks along the Chicago River east of downtown celebrate the New Year and reflect the dazzle of the Chicago skyline.

Left: This plaque from the Chicago Post Office notes the date the city was founded and the city's motto, "Urbs in Horto," meaning city in a garden.

"I feel privileged to live in a city that harmoniously combines the majestic natural beauty of the lakefront with the simple charms of neighborhood life."
—James Sheahan, director of special events for the mayor's office

The sandy beaches and friendly surf that delight Chicagoans from dawn to dusk have inspired some to dub the city "The Third Coast."

Above: An aerial view of North Avenue Beach, one of dozens along Chicago's twenty-nine-mile lakefront, almost all of which belongs to the public. This spit of land hosts popular beach volleyball games all summer long.

Left: With windy Lake Michigan so nearby, sailing is naturally a popular summer pastime. From the internationally recognized Mackinac, the world's oldest and longest freshwater sailing race, held each July, to this fleet of catamarans beached in Olive Park north of Navy Pier, setting sail appeals to a wide variety of people.

> "I tell visitors from China that America is a large country surrounded by Canada, New York, Miami Beach, Texas, and Disneyland; Chicago is the 'Hung Sin,' our country's heart in the heartland of our country."
> —Norman Ross, unofficial city host

Above: A barge on the South Branch of the Chicago River serves as a reminder that this is still a working waterway.

Right: Since the 1970s, Chicago has been rediscovering its river front; new and renovated buildings now face toward the river rather than away from the waterway. Representative of this change is Fulton House (left of the bridge), residential condominiums converted from a cold storage company. Each fall and spring, bridges open for sailboats heading out to or returning from summer moorings on Lake Michigan.

Above: Chicago exists because its river provided access to the heart of the continent, and once the city was established, the Chicago River changed rapidly from meandering stream to major inland port. The trees here mark Wolf Point, home first to Native American encampments, then fur traders, and now the Merchandise Mart's Apparel Center. To the left is 333 W. Wacker Drive, a glass-walled building that mirrors the river's curve and the city's elegance.

Left: Water draining from a pier near North Avenue Beach graciously accents the skyline along North Lake Shore Drive.

"Put the city up; tear the city down;
put it up again.
Let us find a city."
—Carl Sandburg, from
"The Windy City," 1922

23

Above: Monroe Harbor is a peaceful counterpoint to Loop office buildings brightly lit to welcome World Cup participants in June 1994.

Left: With Lake Michigan as its front yard, Chicago offers visual drama from dawn to dusk. Here joggers greet the day along North Lake Shore Drive.

"There is a unique clarity to this great Midwestern city, where relentless winds from the west sweep the sky clean. A neighbor's face, treetops, rooftops, the line where the sky meets the lake—on a typical day, each stands out in crisp precision."
—Alice Sinkevich, architecture association director

Right: A city for all seasons, Chicago welcomes diehard fishermen year round. Navy Pier rewarded this brave soul with a catch on a sunny but frigid day.

Far right: A snowstorm visually softens the boldness of the skyline.

Above: Ice floes lend an Arctic air as frosty skyscrapers rise like icebergs after a winter storm.

Opposite: One of the few structures to survive the Great Chicago Fire of 1871, the Historic Water Tower was originally built to house a 138-foot standpipe that stabilized the water pressure from the adjacent Pumping Station, along what was then the city's lakeshore. Today this popular structure, sitting where Michigan and Chicago Avenues meet, houses one of the city's visitor information centers.

City of Commerce

"This will be the gate of an empire, this will be the seat of commerce. The
typical man who will grow up here must be an enterprising
man. Each day, as he rises, he will exclaim, I act, I move, I push."
—Robert Cavelier, Sieur de La Salle, in 1682 upon visiting
a place Native Americans called "Checagou."

*Above: In 1852, when it had become clear that Chicago was on a major growth curve and lakefront
erosion indicated that the city needed a breakwater, the Illinois Central Railroad offered to construct
one in return for a right of way on a trestle in the lake, along Michigan Avenue to a terminal near the
river. Two decades later, debris from the Great Chicago Fire and the subsequent rebuilding of the Loop
provided landfill between the shore and the tracks, an area that became majestic Grant Park adjacent
to the city center. Today, thousands of commuters still use the IC to come and go from the city via this
nineteenth-century right of way.*

*Opposite: Construction of the Michigan Avenue Bridge in 1920 spurred commercial development north
of the Chicago River. Originally, the Wrigley Building (at left) and Tribune Tower (at right) were promi-
nent anchors of stately "Boul Mich," as the artery was called. Now they blend with a dozen other architectural statements marching up the avenue.*

Above: Chicago's strategically located waterway was the initial reason for the city's existence; its dominance as a port led to the city's becoming a natural hub for the nation's burgeoning rail system in the mid-nineteenth century. Today, air transportion continues that tradition. Sixty-six million travelers move through O'Hare International Airport each year, making it the world's busiest airport.

CREDIT MOVES THE MODERN

BVSINESS WORLD

Above: Named after the French explorer who predicted in 1682 that Chicago would be a "seat of commerce" that would draw "enterprising" men, LaSalle Street honors his prophecy. Financial institutions such as the Chicago Board of Trade, banks, and countless law offices line this canyon of business.

Opposite, bottom left: Chicago-based United Airlines has its own terminal at O'Hare. A creation of Chicago architect Helmut Jahn, the innovative design provides visual excitement as well as easy movement from check-in to gate. In addition, the airport's new Automated People Mover whisks travelers from one terminal to another; the Chicago Transit Authority trains rush them into the city from an airport station.

Opposite, bottom right: The universal commercial sentiment that "Credit Moves the Modern Business World" adorns an office building at Lake and Wells Streets in Chicago's Loop.

31

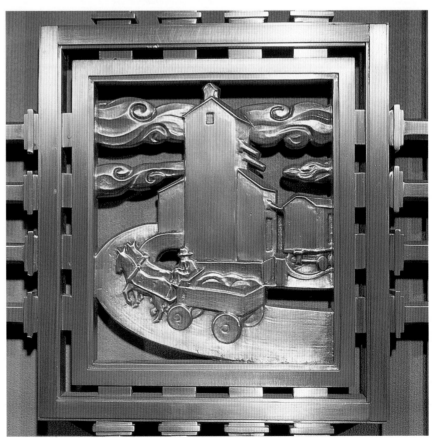

Above: Though computers now dominate many aspects of exchanges, they haven't yet replaced hand signals among the traders in the pits at the Chicago Mercantile Exchange.

Right: A "golden stream" is what the grains first traded on Chicago's exchanges were called. A bronze panel in the Chicago Board of Trade at the foot of LaSalle Street recalls the mutually reinforcing relationship between farmers, who brought their grain to rural elevators to be shipped to the city, and traders in Chicago, who turned it into money. Trains brought the grain into the city and shipped out lumber and other goods to build farms and towns on the prairies.

Left: In 1893, famed architect Louis Sullivan designed a building for the Chicago Stock Exchange; in 1972 developers decided that his exquisite creation was no longer the best use of its site at Washington and LaSalle. The building's demolition (and replacement by a nondescript structure) became a clarion call for preservation of the city's other architectural treasures. The relocated entrance arch of the exchange (pictured here) now graces the grounds of the Art Institute. Behind the arch, located on Columbus Drive, looms the Amoco Building, second tallest in the city and one of the ten tallest in the world.

"We're a city of risk-takers. By the time the experts tell us, 'It can't be done,' we have already succeeded beyond our wildest expectations and even moved ahead to the next step, but at the same time, we've developed and perfected institutions for managing risk—the futures exchanges. Here, first farmers, producers, and ranchers, then later, entrepreneurs, businesses, and financial institutions the world over have come to ensure that their hard-earned financial gains don't fall prey to economic uncertainties."
—Carol Sexton, futures exchange executive

Above: A bronze statue of Diana (goddess of the hunt) caps the headquarters of Montgomery Ward along the Chicago River at Chicago Avenue. According to company founder Aaron Montgomery Ward, Diana symbolizes "commerce leading to progress." With Sears, Roebuck and a host of other companies, Ward made Chicago the mail-order shopping center of the world during the first half of the twentieth century.

Left: Originally built as headquarters for Marshall Field and Company's wholesale operations, the 1930 Merchandise Mart was acquired by Joseph P. Kennedy in 1945. Now home to the Chicago World Trade Center, its 4.1 million square feet of wholesale showrooms make it the largest commercial building in the world, and it is still owned by the Kennedy family. Fur traders camped out two centuries ago on Wolf Point, in the foreground.

"Chicago is practical and not off-the-wall. The city makes sense. Things are accessible and it's easy to get around for both business and entertainment. But most of all, I like the people here. They aren't full of a lot of talk, but are people of considerable action. Things get accomplished here. There is a certain pulse in this city not to be found anywhere else in the U.S."
—Joanne Bongiorno, public relations director

Michigan Avenue south of Randolph Street was Chicago's most prestigious residential street in the city's first decades; later it became a prime office address. Buildings by famed turn-of-the-century architect and planner Daniel Burnham, head of design for the 1893 World's Columbian Exposition and the chief author of the 1909 Plan of Chicago, still dominate the avenue. A grand design for Grant Park, along the downtown lakeshore, was among his ideas for the city. Pictured here is a tulip garden in the park just south of Jackson Boulevard.

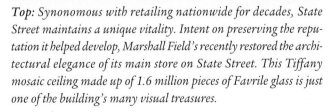

Top: Synonomous with retailing nationwide for decades, State Street maintains a unique vitality. Intent on preserving the reputation it helped develop, Marshall Field's recently restored the architectural elegance of its main store on State Street. This Tiffany mosaic ceiling made up of 1.6 million pieces of Favrile glass is just one of the building's many visual treasures.

Above: Trendsetting Crate & Barrel has continued Chicago's tradition of innovative retailing. Its flagship store, built in 1990, follows the movement of upscale emporiums to North Michigan Avenue, while its strongly modernist design asserts its own interpretation of the avenue's architectural conventions.

Moorish details decorate this pool (allegedly where Johnny Weissmuller trained for his role as Tarzan) in the Hotel Inter-Continental on North Michigan Avenue. Built as the Medinah Athletic Club in 1929, this architectural fantasy incorporates Egyptian, Assyrian, Celtic, Medieval, and Spanish influences and is a testament to the prosperity and aspirations of its founding members (who were also responsible for the nearby Medinah Temple, a similarly inspired confection). Alas, the Depression hit these bourgeois boosters hard, and the building foundered until its lavish 1990 restoration by the Inter-Continental chain.

Above: The Rookery Building takes its name from a brief period right after the Chicago fire when the city hall was located here. Pigeons had made it a favorite roost; hence the name. Originally designed by the firm of Burnham and Root in the late 1880s, the Rookery's light court and lobbies were renovated in 1905 by Frank Lloyd Wright. Street signs embellishing a building's corner were a standard practice when the Rookery was built. Fortunately, these were not modernized away.

Right: The Rookery was elegantly restored in 1992. This roofline detail just hints at the majesty of the interior.

"I see Chicago as distinguished by three dominant characteristics: ambition, energy, and generosity. Ambition has, since the beginning, brought people to Chicago from all parts of the world—ambition to make money with which to provide a better life for their families than they had elsewhere. And Chicagoans have the energy to carry out their ambitions. The city's streets are vibrant with the energy of its citizens hurrying about their business. As for generosity, I have had occasion to observe this heart-warming quality in hundreds of ways, meeting a multitude of people who give of their time and talents for quite incommensurate returns."
—Mary Ward Wolkonsky, civic leader extraordinaire

Above: *Details represent the richness of the visual landmark commissioned by chewing-gum magnate William Wrigley, Jr., when the Michigan Avenue Bridge was under construction. Here is a close-up view of the Wrigley Building's bronze detailing above one of its doors.*

Left: *Revolutionary War martyr Nathan Hale guards one entrance to the Tribune Tower, home of the Chicago Tribune and WGN (for the self-described "world's greatest newspaper") radio. Completed shortly after the Wrigley Building across Michigan Avenue, the Tribune Tower's Gothic design was the winner of an international competition.*

"Make no little plans; they have no magic to stir men's blood and probably themselves will not be realized. Make big plans; aim high in hope and work, remembering that a noble, logical diagram once recorded will never die, but long after we are gone will be a living thing, asserting itself with ever-growing intensity. Remember that our sons and grandsons are going to do things that would stagger us. Let your watchword be order and your beacon beauty."
—Daniel H. Burnham, visionary and turn-of-the-century architect and planner

Above: The glass skin of 333 W. Wacker eloquently reflects the city's moods. Named for civic leader Charles H. Wacker, who spearheaded the implementation of the 1909 Plan of Chicago, Wacker Drive curves here alongside the South Branch of the Chicago River. The two-tiered drive was designed to carry heavy commercial traffic on its lower level, automobiles and pedestrians on the upper level.

Right: The 1969 John Hancock Center towers above the rest of the North Michigan Avenue skyline, which is seen here across the bustling office and gallery district known as River North. Fazlur L. Khan, who later helped erect the Sears Tower, was also responsible for the engineering innovations that made "Big John" possible. Diagonal cross bracing supports its tapering form.

Above: The holiday spirit is seen through the windows of the arch-shaped west entrance addition to the Sears Tower at the southern end of Wacker Drive. A new skydeck entrance on Van Buren Street makes the tower more visitor friendly.

Left: The Sears Tower, completed in 1974, dominates the Chicago skyline from every direction. The view here is from a combined office and residential neighborhood just west of the Loop.

"Enchanting . . . there is no more livable major business community in the world."
—Paul D. Astleford,
convention bureau director

Above: The North Michigan Avenue area appears more human-scaled in this view from the Gold Coast, which begins on the avenue's northern edge. Chicago's resurgent commercial strength was repeatedly asserted during the 1980s building boom. When that decade began, about the only notable structures between the Hancock Center (at left) and the Sears Tower (at right) were the corncob-shaped twin towers of Marina City (just right of center). Today, these skyscrapers are joined by a dozen other formidable structures.

"Chicago is a place of possibilities, a place for making fresh starts. I think it always has been. It is a place where people with dreams and ideas can make things happen if they want. It's a place where you find out soon enough that to get things you want done, you need people, a lot of them, and that makes you get involved."

—Albert Friedman,
real estate developer

The stores on the Magnificent Mile now lure an estimated fifteen to twenty million shoppers annually. In 1983, a branch of Texas-based Neiman Marcus chose a site just south of Chicago Avenue. The entrance honors the arches favored by architect Louis Sullivan (see the entrance arch of the former Chicago Stock Exchange building on page 33).

Christmas comes to Bloomingdale's, anchor store of an eight-level mall at 900 N. Michigan Avenue. In Chicago's mixed-use tradition, this building also includes office space and the elegant Four Seasons Hotel, along with several restaurants and a movie theater.

Had the 1909 Plan of Chicago been fully realized, the site of this building along the Eisenhower Expressway west of the Loop would have been a grand civic center. This trompe-l'oeil mural by Richard Haas, completed in 1984, recalls this grand dream of the past and offers the artist's vision of the Sears Tower at the corner. Visible in the distance is the imposing structure of the real thing. Nine independent but mutually supporting column-free square shafts enable the building to soar taller than any other. Two of these square towers stop at the fiftieth floor, two more at the sixty-sixth, and three others at the ninetieth. The final two rise the building's full 110 stories.

The proximity to Lake Michigan was responsible for Chicago's initial growth; it can also be blamed for the dense fog that occasionally settles over downtown. The city, emboldened by a conviction that it could defy nature by raising structures out of a swamp, reversing the course of a river, and building higher than anyone had ever gone before, can be subdued by the very nature that made it possible in the first place.

City of Culture

"Chicagoans occupy the same place in the world of city dwellers
that humans do in the world of animals. We are not the swiftest
nor the slowest, not the most dangerous nor the most peaceful, but
a highly effective mixture of the best qualities of our world. . . .
Another good thing about Chicagoans is that when we say, 'let's
have lunch,' we generally mean that a meal will be eaten."
—Aaron Freeman, actor, comedian, radio & TV host

Above: The recently re-energized Chicago Cultural Center, built in 1897 as the Chicago Public Library on Michigan Avenue between Randolph and Washington, has assumed its place as one of the cultural icons of the city. This imposing statue of another icon, entitled Young Lincoln, *graces an exhibition hall in the Cultural Center, which also houses a startlingly fresh and constantly changing array of free art exhibits throughout the year.*

Opposite: One Financial Plaza on South LaSalle Street is the site of Ludovico de Luigi's magnificent bronze, San Marco II. *This nine-foot-high horse in mid-stride is de Luigi's salute to the eleventh-century horse sculptures that once graced the facade of St. Mary's Basilica on the Piazza San Marco in his native Venice.*

Dedicated in 1927, Buckingham Fountain was a gift to the city by Kate Sturges Buckingham, whose family, having made its fortune in grain trading, was also a major donor to the Art Institute of Chicago. The fountain's 1.5 million gallons of water skyrocket 140 feet in the air above Grant Park, and its evening light shows fascinate natives and visitors.

Above left: Props from "Kukla, Fran and Ollie," one of the early children's television shows broadcast from Chicago, recalls the city's pioneering role in the development of radio and television. This exhibit is one of many found in the Museum of Broadcast Communications inside the Chicago Cultural Center.

Above: Among Chicago's many contributions to music and drama is the idea that commercial real estate could subsidize opera and concert performances if both were housed in the same building. Hence, the 1889 Auditorium Theatre (the architectural firm of Adler and Sullivan's first major commission) and the 1929 Civic Opera Building on South Wacker Drive were built. Pictured here is the Auditorium's box office lobby, a lovely entrance hall with marble walls, art glass over the door, and an inlaid marble floor.

Left: The Chicago Cultural Center's marble and mosaic grand stairway merely suggests the visual splendor inside. Don't miss Preston Bradley Hall upstairs where free concerts are offered each Wednesday at noon under a Tiffany-inspired dome of Favrile glass.

"Chicago has a robust, slap you on the back, take it all in stride spirit. If others try us; they like us.
The flaw—there has to be a flaw—is that Chicagoans are mostly unaware of the history that made them. Undaunted, that muse seeps into our collective unconscious as we look at the grand front yard park that is built on the debris of a devastating fire, or as our daily lives are shaped by the height, the grandeur, or the brick utility of a built environment praising prairie democracy."
—Jean Hunt, Chicago historian and author

Chicago philanthropists have endowed a long tradition of public sculpture; their subjects reflect their times. This commemoration of the Fort Dearborn Massacre, which occurred when unrest during the War of 1812 forced settlers to evacuate Chicago, reflects an earlier time. Originally on display at the Chicago Historical Society, it now sits in the Prairie Avenue Historic District on 18th Street, not far from where the event it depicts took place.

Guarding the Art Institute's entrance since 1894, sculptor Edward Kemys's lions have become cultural icons themselves. In a celebration of Chicago's dual identity of spectacular sports and high culture, they were decorated recently with caps and helmets to salute the Bulls' three NBA championships and the Bears' Superbowl win. One wonders if they'll roar should the Cubs or Sox bring home a World Series title.

Jerry Peart's Splash rises whimsically on the plaza of the modernist Illinois Center on Michigan Avenue just south of the Chicago River. The dark green and gold terracotta shaft of the 1929 Carbide and Carbon Building towers across the street.

Above: Visitors to the Art Institute of Chicago admiring earlier admirers of Gustave Caillebotte's Paris Street; Rainy Day. Along with Georges Seurat's A Sunday on La Grand Jatte-1884, *Caillebotte's painting is a familiar part of the museum's Impressionist collection, often praised as second only in comprehensiveness and quality to the Louvre in Paris.*

Left: The garden restaurant of the Art Institute offers a pleasant oasis for dining on a July day and hosts standing-room-only crowds for jazz concerts on Tuesday nights during the summer months. Carl Milles's Triton Fountain *is its centerpiece.*

"Chicago to me is talk show; though it's a town that's been known for 'doing'—handling freight and forging steel, stacking wheat and butchering hogs, trading futures and scraping the sky, Chicago best expresses itself to those who listen. It's no surprise that the 'Oprah Winfrey Show,' arguably the most popular TV talk show in the nation, is broadcast from Chicago, or that Studs Terkel, Chicago's 'recording angel,' as one writer described him, is able to get people to talk so honestly about things that matter to them. For years, the city boasted a platform for free speech in Washington Square; known as Bughouse Square, it was Chicago's answer to the speaker's corner in London's Hyde Park. Step into a cab, have your hair cut, order a cappuccino, or just walk down the street today—just listen or add a few words of your own—and you become part of a city that talks."
—Kristina Valaitis, humanities council director

Right: The significance of mercantile fortunes to commerce and culture in Chicago is well expressed by the institutions that grace a promontory into Lake Michigan south of Grant Park. The Field Museum of Natural History and the John G. Shedd Aquarium were gifts made possible by the wealth Marshall Field and Company generated; the Max Adler Planetarium here and the Museum of Science and Industry on the south side were likewise made possible by Sears, Roebuck. The first planetarium in the Western hemisphere when it opened in 1930, the Adler still sets precedents with its shows of the stars, planets, and night sky. Following the last show each Friday evening, spectators enjoy views from outer space transmitted directly into the theater from the Planetarium's Doane Observatory. The Adler's twelve-sided building represents the signs of the zodiac, and Henry Moore's Sundial *accents the plaza in front.*

Below: Built originally as the Palace of Fine Arts for the 1893 World's Columbian Exposition, the Museum of Science and Industry reopened in its present use at the time of the 1933 Century of Progress Exposition. The building also housed the Field Museum of Natural History for twenty-five years. The Museum of Science and Industry is one of the many benefactions of Julius Rosenwald, the Sears, Roebuck president responsible for the company's long hold on the nation's taste and pocketbooks, and it is a sentimental favorite of many Chicagoans.

Left top: The Shedd Aquarium is also a pioneering institution. Nearly two hundred tanks containing thousands of specimens radiate out from the popular Coral Reef exhibit, particularly fascinating when divers enter daily to feed the fish. The Shedd's Oceanarium, completed in 1991, contains the world's largest indoor sea world, an exhibit that approximates the Alaskan coastline.

Left bottom: Pictured here is the Museum of Science and Industry's new transportation exhibit "Take Flight," featuring a Boeing 727. The annual "Christmas Trees From Around the World" exhibit is in the background. Other long-time favorite exhibits here include the fairy castle, coal mine, old-fashioned Main Street, and U-505 submarine.

"What I find most unique and exciting about Chicago is how wonderful it is to be able to actually *live* in the heart of the city. I can watch the sun rise over the lake each morning or see the holiday fireworks from my apartment window. I can walk to Marshall Field's or to a Bears game at Soldier Field, Buckingham Fountain, sidewalk cafes, the Grant Park rose garden, and the exciting museums in downtown Chicago —all richly rewarding urban living experiences."
—Barbara Lynne, civic leader

Monumental Stanley Field Hall dominates the Field Museum's main floor. Completed in 1920, the museum is dedicated to exploring diverse physical environments and cultures and has revitalized its vast collections by organizing them in more people-friendly exhibits. Hence, such sensory learning experiences as "Inside Ancient Egypt" and "Traveling the Pacific" have emerged.

Above: A mere half century after Henry Ives Cobb created the University of Chicago's campus and Frank Lloyd Wright designed the Robie House, another preeminent force in modern architecture, Ludwig Mies van der Rohe, created Crown Hall, perhaps the largest one-room school house ever built. In the mid-1930s, the Armour Institute, which later merged with another institution to become the Illinois Institute of Technology, lured Mies to head its school of architecture. Already well established in Europe for his revolutionary insistence that "less is more," he had a profound effect on American architecture—the strict geometry of glass-walled skyscrapers, which dominated urban skylines at mid-century and later, were inspired by Mies. The IIT campus near Comiskey Park on Chicago's south side was designed by him, and the 1956 Crown Hall houses the school of architecture he once chaired.

Left top: In the 1920s, while Mies was working with glass and geometry in Germany and Wright was flirting with Japanese architecture in California, Chicago firms were more comfortable with the neo-classical influence that Daniel Burnham helped popularize with his design for the World's Columbian Exposition. Typical of this influence, a goddess figure and Corinthian columns grace the entry to 360 N. Michigan Avenue. This 1923 building and 333 N. Michigan, an Art Deco beauty across the avenue, are architectural complements to the Wrigley Building and Tribune Tower directly across the Chicago River.

Left bottom: Opened in 1891 with a major grant from John D. Rockefeller, the University of Chicago soon established itself as one of the world's premier research institutions. Henry Ives Cobb's neo-Gothic architecture dominates the main quadrangle of the Hyde Park campus. Other highlights of the campus include the Oriental Institute, Smart Museum, Rockefeller Chapel, and the nearby Robie House.

"Let this building be the home of ideas and adventure [that would be] in the end a real contribution to our civilization."
—Ludwig Mies van der Rohe
at the 1956 dedication of Crown Hall

Opposite top: The Robie House in Hyde Park, built in 1909 and designed by Frank Lloyd Wright, was designated a National Historic Landmark in 1963 and is a must see for architecture aficionados. Predominant features of the Prairie style he helped define include earth-hugging horizontal lines, reminiscent of the midwestern landscape; natural materials; exquisite detailing with wood and leaded glass (barely visible under the wide, protective eaves); and sympathetic interaction between the interior and the outdoors.

Opposite bottom left: Banker and real estate investor Walter Loomis Newberry stipulated in his will that, should his two daughters have no heirs, half of his fortune should be used to endow a library. Both women died young of tuberculosis, and in 1893 the Newberry Library was constructed on Walton Street a few blocks west of North Michigan Avenue. Its extraordinary collection, open to the public, is particularly strong in cartography, Native American studies, genealogy, and the Renaissance.

Opposite bottom right: The Chicago Historical Society is a few blocks north of the Newberry and has anchored the southwest corner of Lincoln Park since 1932. Artifacts representing various aspects of Chicago history flank its entrance, and regularly changing exhibits emphasize Chicago themes. The Society's library is open to the public, and its bookstore offers a wondrous assortment of Chicago memorabilia.

Right top: Dedicated to the memory of Chicago's first African American mayor, the Harold Washington Library Center became the new home for Chicago's main library in 1991. Its design, selected from an architectural competition, remains controversial; architectural purists regard the soaring roofline ornament as "decorative overkill." Nevertheless, the Harold Washington Library Center brings new liveliness to the once dreary intersection of State Street and Congress Parkway. Intriguing exhibits, extensive contemporary art holdings, and a growing collection of books make it worth a visit.

Right bottom: Even more controversial is the James R. Thompson (originally the State of Illinois) Center, named after the longtime governor who commissioned it from architect Helmut Jahn. Cost overruns and its assertive shape drew criticism before it opened, then heating and cooling the glass-ceilinged curiosity proved an engineering challenge. Yet, visitors are fascinated by its soaring atrium. Jean Dubuffet's whimsical Monument with Standing Beast *animates the building's entrance along Randolph Street. The classically inspired R. R. Donnelley Building two blocks north soars in the background.*

55

Above: In past generations, public art and sculpture tended to celebrate famous people. Today, it more often celebrates itself. Examples abound outdoors and inside buildings throughout Chicago, and much of it has been made possible by the Percent for Art Program, which is managed by the Department of Cultural Affairs and mandates that 1.3 percent of the cost of all public buildings must go to commission art to decorate them. All year long, passersby on the sidewalks in front of Marshall Field's State Street store can contemplate Chicagoan Virgino Ferrari's "Being Born," situated under the store's famed clock. Commissioned by the tool and die industry—still a major Chicago trade—Ferrari's piece celebrates the precision and skill these metal fabricators bring to their work. Its two stainless steel elements fit precisely into each other.

Left: And then there's Chicago's Picasso, which the artist didn't name when he created it and no one else has since it arrived at the Civic Center Plaza (now named after the late Mayor Richard J. Daley) in 1967. It is the subject of endless debate—is it a woman, a bird, or something else entirely? Though skateboarding its sloping base is officially forbidden, the challenge has become a rite of passage for the city's young people. More sedate folks gather under the Picasso for frequent noontime performances and a popular Farmer's Market each summer.

Inventor of the "stabile," or stationary mobile, American sculptor Alexander Calder was trained both as an engineer and an artist. Though firmly attached to the Federal Center Plaza on South Dearborn Street, his 1974 Flamingo (above) looks capable of walking away. Calder's wall sculpture, Universe, (left) from the same year, enlivens the Sears Tower lobby a few blocks away.

"I've traveled the world, and I often say that I was born in New York and reborn in Chicago!"
—Bill Harnett, founder of a popular tourist attraction

Above: For decades, Chicago civic leaders debated what to do with the dilapidating Navy Pier. Turning its fifty acres into parks, gardens, shops, theaters, restaurants, a museum, and exhibition spaces to appeal to natives and conventioneers was the agreed-upon solution. During the summer of 1994, Skyline Stage, the first of these attractions, opened. Highlighted against the Chicago skyline, it's a delicious place to spend a summer evening.

"Chicago is a special city. It's a sophisticated city with friendly people, lively culture, clean streets, and diverse and wonderful restaurants. Chicago is home to the bulls and the bears, where the B's are both uppercase and lowercase. Chicago is a melange of ethnicities that keep it vibrant. Chicago is where potholes get fixed just once every four years, immediately before mayoral elections, and taxes get raised just once every four years, immediately after mayoral elections. And Chicago is Lake Michigan, a wonder to see as it changes from turbulent waves to peaceful whitecaps, sometimes in just a few hours."

—Sandye Wexler, travel store owner

Built in 1921, the 3,800-seat Chicago Theater was a marvel of its age, a time when movie theaters were palatial. Then, changing public tastes rendered these lavish showhouses outdated, and demolition began. Fortunately, a group of civic-minded citizens organized to restore this gem in the mid-1980s. Now managed by the nonprofit Civic Preservation Foundation, the theater continues to attract big-name, live entertainment.

The Biograph on North Lincoln Avenue still operates as a theater for first-run films. It achieved notoriety in 1934 as the site where FBI agents shot and killed gangster John Dillinger, a setup arranged by his unfaithful girlfriend, who was in cahoots with the feds.

Along with the Chicago Symphony Orchestra, the Lyric Opera draws international talent and sellout audiences. The Lyric is also noted for staging some of current opera's most innovative productions. Pictured here is a surreal scene from its 1994 production of Igor Stravinsky's "The Rake's Progress." (Photo © John Reilly/Lyric Opera of Chicago)

Venues for jazz and blues are not limited to downtown. Taking the stage at City Limits in Edgewater on the north side is singer Gloria Jean Shannon.

Along with the Bulls, Bears, and Blackhawks, the blues are synonymous with Chicago. "Skaggs," blues singer Pat Soul, belted it out at popular venue Blue Chicago when it opened a second club on Clark Street near Chicago Avenue.

Above left: *The original Regal Theater on Chicago's south side was once a showplace for talents like Duke Ellington, Lena Horne, and Nat King Cole. Unfortunately, over the years that building succumbed to neglect and was demolished. But in 1977, a citizens' group acquired a distinguished movie theater not far away and restored it to become the New Regal Theater. Calvin Jones was commissioned to create this mural on the theater's exterior, which salutes black artists, including "Moms" Mabley and Ray Charles, among others.*

Above right: *The blues may have been born in the Mississippi Delta, but Muddy Waters and Howlin' Wolf brought them to the streets of Chicago. A vintage bus parked at the New Maxwell Street Market proclaims this heritage*

"For an adventurous person, steadfastly armed with a city map and the Yellow Pages, who is perpetually in search of superb bargains, outlet stores, antique shops, unique businesses, arts happenings, and who is always in a hurry . . . there's nothing like Chicago's diagonal streets and Lower Wacker Drive. My favorites are Clybourn . . . to take you to the Crate & Barrel Outlet Store and Whole Foods. Elston takes you to Alice Berry Designs, Stanley's Fruits and Vegetables, Handy Andy's, and Edward Don's restaurant supply. Milwaukee Avenue takes you to ethnic restaurants, artists' studios, galleries, and theaters—and, alas, in the good old days—nothing got you from Lincoln Park to the University of Illinois at Chicago any faster than Ogden. Need to get to the Lyric or the main post office from Columbus Drive? Lower Wacker Drive in a flash! Whatta city!!"
—Madeline Murphy Rabb, arts consultant

City at Play

"Chicago's style is unique because there isn't any. In dress, food, media, the arts, even business, Chicago doesn't care what's trendy, hip, hot, or chic elsewhere. . . . This 'free style' is tremendously liberating, since no one cares what you do. . . . And then there are the lakefront and skyline, making Chicago the world's most beautiful flat city."
—Jonathan Abarbanel, theater critic

Above: Shoppers purusing goods offered at the Printer's Row Book Fair held each June in the South Loop neighborhood that was once home to the city's printers.

Opposite: At night, the Ferris wheel at the Taste of Chicago brightens the skyline over Grant Park.

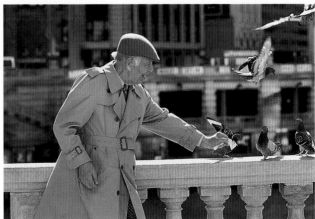

*Style or no style, Chicago offers many and varied ways to amuse oneself, both organized and spontaneous. A sampling of opportunities in the city include **(top)** a weekend visit to Lincoln Park Zoo; **(above left)** welcoming the New Year in Chinatown, just minutes away from the Loop; **(above right)** feeding pigeons on a bridge over the Chicago River; and **(opposite)** performing—or appreciating—skateboarder acrobatics in Daley Plaza across from City Hall.*

Right: Native prairie grasses mix with the blooms of summer in this Grant Park garden just east of South Michigan Avenue.

Below: One of Chicago's annual rites of spring is the smelt run in Lake Michigan. Each April, the allure of netting these tiny, silver-skinned delicacies draws standing-room-only crowds of anglers to piers throughout the city. The season begins anew at dusk each day. Here, smelt-season devotees have Shedd Aquarium's Oceanarium as backdrop.

Left: Fall means football practice all over the country, but only in Chicago can it be held in the ubiquitous presence of the Sears Tower. Here, the Mustangs of Dunbar High School south of the Loop get ready for a game.

Complaining about cold weather is popular in Chicago, but without winter there would be no (**above**) sledding at dusk in Warren Park on the northwest side, (**right**) ice fishing in Burnham Harbor south of the Loop, (**far right**) or Skate on State. The latter is an artificial rink in the heart of downtown. In 1990, the site was cleared of several historically significant buildings for a shopping and office complex. Development stalled nationwide that year, and the project was never constructed, so several civic groups got together to put this city-owned land to public use. In the summer, it is an outdoor art school for city high school students. Plug Bug, an oversize painting by Chicago artist Karl Wirsum, enlivens a substation that brings electricity to area offices.

"This is the best city in the world. The only reason we have bad weather is to discourage people from moving here."
—Oprah Winfrey, actress and television personality

Above: Chicago and Rio de Janeiro are possibly the world's only major cities where sandy beaches mix so well with exclusive real estate. Bathers in the Midwest, however, dress a bit more modestly. The fortunate residents of East Lake Shore Drive, the city's toniest address, can run across the street for a swim at Oak Street Beach. Others have to travel farther, and they do; on steamy summer Sundays, latecomers find bare patches of sand as scarce as snowballs.

Left: North Avenue's Chess Pavilion, a half mile north of Oak Street Beach, offers more cerebral amusement, even on chilly days. Kibitzers and players alike represent all the city's ethnic groups.

"I think I love most the sights and sounds of the city as I drive the length of Lake Shore Drive. This is where I work and play and the very drive brings back a lifetime of memories."
—Karen Kline, Chicago souvenir shops owner

Though all diners at the Signature Room in the John Hancock Center aren't fortunate enough to get the corner tables, it is not possible to find a place without a striking view from atop the third tallest building in Chicago. Visitors with less time—or wherewithal—can visit "Big John's" sky-high cocktail lounge or observation deck.

Chicago is known for ribs as well. Helping that reputation is Leon's Bar-B-Q, three south-side eateries established by Leon Finney, Sr. This one is on 79th Street across from the New Regal Theater.

As the sign above its window recalls, the Billy Goat Tavern's fame spread beyond the Chicago press corps with the "cheezborger, cheezborger" skit on "Saturday Night Live." Regulars at this hangout on lower Michigan Avenue (near the Sun-Times and Tribune buildings) include Mike Royko and other popular columnists.

The city's contributions to the nation's culinary heritage include deep-dish pizza, the flaming-cheese saganaki offered at many Greektown restaurants, and the Chicago Hot Dog, a concoction spiced with onions, tomatoes, and hot peppers. This high-flying (but inedible) version adorns a West Loop eatery.

A diner in the discount shopping area at Canal Street and Roosevelt Road southwest of the Loop offers no-fuss meals.

Summer in the city is celebrated with the annual Taste of Chicago extravaganza in Grant Park, the world's largest annual outdoor food fair. After a week of overindulging on samples from restaurants all over the city, celebrants enjoy the Grant Park Orchestra and a finale of fireworks to welcome the Fourth of July. Since the event draws a million people, Chicago cops are on hand to assure some semblance of order. Here two take a break to fortify themselves.

"Chicago is an amazingly open city. I had an incredible lesson in this, just a few months after moving here to study journalism at Northwestern. The late Richard J. Daley had recently been elected mayor, and I was assigned to attend his morning press conference. After the City Hall reporters had their turn, the mayor asked if a student had any questions. Taken aback, I replied, 'I did, Mr. Mayor, but you squelched it when you said you wouldn't discuss a certain campaign contribution.' The mayor bristled and responded, 'You come to my office at noon.' So there I was, sitting where few reporters from Chicago's then four newspapers got to sit, getting a 45-minute off-the-record lecture about city politics and the press. I asked myself, 'What am I doing here sitting face to face with the venerable mayor of the second largest city in the United States?'. . . By design, but mainly by happenstance, a person can mingle in many circles here."
—Alfred Borcover, travel writer

*From the Great Chicago Fire until the death of Mayor Richard J. Daley, the city's politicians were predominantly Irish. On St. Patrick's Day, everyone is. The celebration begins with turning the Chicago River green (the dye is an orangey red before it hits the water). When the parade sets off, kilted pipers play, colleens smile, and every politician in town marches, regardless of political persuasion or ethnic background. **Below:** The current Mayor Richard M. Daley (at center, in the black overcoat with the green sash) waves his ungloved hand to constituents from the front line of the march.*

Above: Chicago civic boosters have long wished the city would be recognized for something other than Al Capone, and the celestially talented Michael Jordan granted that wish. Jordan, soaring in bronze, characteristically drives for a basket at the main entrance to the new United Center.

Above right: The late afternoon sun bathes the one side of Soldier Field (named to honor World War I casualties) in warm sunshine. Though its classical grandeur is marred by skyboxes, they have helped make the Chicago Bears a financial winner for owner Mike McCaskey, grandson of founder "Papa" George Halas.

"The uniqueness of Chicago can be summed up in four words: it's large, but liveable. It has everything one could want, be it business, sports, culture, adventure, or beauty. All of its attractions are easily accessible to all of its residents. Its lakefront is open and clear and available to everybody. Its transit systems, both mass and highway, ensure accessibility with their efficiency and availability. And finally, the neighborhoods of Chicago are its greatest strength providing enclaves of comfortable living conditions within the hustle and bustle of an urban environment."
—Charlie Gardner, real estate developer

Ivy-lined walls make Wrigley Field a lovely place to be. Despite the Cub's perennial, break-your-heart record, the fans keep coming. Residents of nearby apartment buildings throw rooftop, game-time parties overlooking the outfield (and frequently charge handsomely for the privilege of attending).

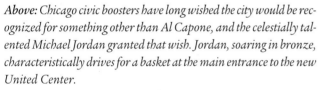

No longer the only major league stadium without night baseball, Wrigley Field still maintains old-fashioned charm with its quaint scoreboard and real greenery. Since 1990, Cub fans have been able to gather at dusk on opening day. Team owner The Chicago Tribune Company, interested in greater advertising revenue from broadcasting the games at night, battled neighborhood residents for years before winning the right to light the field for play after dark.

Chicago traditionally has been split between South Siders and North Siders. While the latter have tended to be Cubs fans, the former have rooted for the White Sox. Though Sox fans have given the new Comiskey Park, completed in 1991, mixed reviews, it has been a solid revenue generator for club owner Jerry Reinsdorf, who grew up a Dodgers fan in Brooklyn and also owns the Chicago Bulls.

City of Neighborhoods

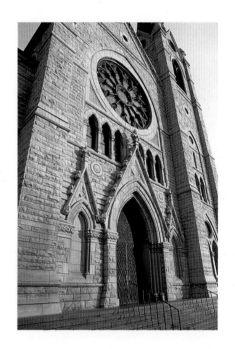

City of Neighborhoods, Chicago proudly asserts, and rightly so. This great capital of the nation's Heartland is the most ethnically balanced major city in the nation, and ever since the election of the late Harold Washington, Chicago's first African American mayor, even the city's political structure reflects its diversity. Originally a city of New Englanders and German immigrants, Chicago later attracted countless others from Ireland and from central and eastern Europe, including many Jews from Russia and Poland. In addition, scatterings of Greeks, Italians, Swedes, and Lithuanians found their way to Chicago around the turn of the century. In the first half of this century, Chicago became a mecca for African Americans from Mississippi; later Mexican laborers came to the city. More recently, the city has attracted immigrants from India, Korea, and Vietnam. Chicago's neighborhoods, particularly their churches, tell the history of immigrant groups moving in, through, and out of the city.

Above right: Holy Name Cathedral, an imposing, Gothic structure on North State Street, has been the home parish of Chicago's Catholic cardinals since 1875. Though notable weddings and funerals have taken place here, among the most familiar stories associated with it are the 1926 slaughter of gangster Hymie Weiss on its steps and the 1924 murder of fellow mobster Dion O'Banion in his flower shop across the street.

Opposite: Since the city was platted, the Lincoln Park neighborhood has drawn prosperous residents. Wood frame houses surrounded by white picket fences filled the area a century ago. The residential streets were later lined with brick and limestone townhouses. In the 1920s, lakeshore mansions were replaced with elegant apartment buildings; several line Lincoln Park West across from the Lincoln Park Conservatory. The conservatory's outdoor gardens include the delightful Bates Fountain by Augustus Saint-Gaudens and his assistant, Frederick MacMonnies.

Above: *In 1882, business and society leaders Potter and Bertha Palmer orchestrated construction of their red-brick palace on North Lake Shore Drive. Over the next two decades, Chicago's aristocracy followed them north from Prairie Avenue. This holiday-decorated doorway on East Bellevue Place, near where the Palmers's mansion once stood, epitomizes the splendid residential showplaces that soon gave the near-north Gold Coast its name.*

Above right: *The heritage of Pilsen, a community on the city's lower west side, has a far more varied history. A staunchly Czech area beginning in the 1870s, it has become the center of Chicago's Mexican community. The afternoon sun catches the smiling faces of these young Pilsen residents.*

Right: *On the near northwest side, Poles long dominated; Chicago has the largest number of Polish residents of any city other than Warsaw. In 1979, artist and Little Polonia resident Edwin Szewczyk began adorning the front of his house with this paean to film stars that he's dubbed "It's What I Do." Chicago has always taken great pride in its iconoclasts.*

Left top: Old Town was first populated by Italian immigrants and then by Germans. Beginning in the late 1950s, the area became popular with artists, hippies, and other bohemians. The Old Town Art Fair, a popular summertime institution, closes off the streets of this now-gentrified neighborhood every year. This is Wells Street, the neighborhood's main shopping area.

Left bottom: Another bit of Chicago folklore concerns self-designated Captain George Wellington Streeter who claimed that much of the area surrounding the spot where his boat ran aground on a sandbar in 1886—then a few hundred yards out in Lake Michigan—was his, not part of the city; a thirty-plus year battle with the city ensued until he was finally evicted. Now one of the most densely populated and upscale neighborhoods in the city, Streeterville is filled with elegant highrises. A few gracious townhouses, built on neighborhood land the good captain didn't claim, remain from his era.

"I love Chicago for very personal, geographic reasons. Today, I work only six blocks away from where I was born. When I go up to the seventh floor of our building, I can see the steeple of St. Michael's Church, where I went to grade school. My office is on Rush Street. When I was a young single guy, this was the nightlife hotspot, and I hung out several nights a week there. One block from my office is Holy Name Cathedral. I was married there. Our first apartment was in Old Town, and from there we could still hear the bells of St. Michael's. As an old friend once chided me,
'You haven't come far in all these years, have you?' No, but I didn't have to."
—Joe Cappo, newspaper publisher and columnist

For a century, railroads filled Chicago's near south side. In the 1950s, it began to languish as airlines and highways replaced trains. But today, it's evolved into a popular residential area. Highlights include Dearborn Station (opposite page) and River City, another mixed-use development by architect Bertrand Goldberg. Like his Marina City on the Chicago River's north bank, which sparked a return to downtown living, this one combines residential, retail, and commercial functions—along with a marina.

Above: An El train passes through Rush-Presbyterian-Saint Luke's in the background. The University of Illinois Medical School, Cook County Hospital, and the West Side Veterans Hospital are among the many medical institutions headquartered here.

Left: The 1885 Dearborn Station (originally called Polk Street Station) represents the neighborhood's past and present. Once a major terminal, it is now a commercial building linking Printer's Row, a lively area of converted loft apartments, with Dearborn Park, a new and semisuburban residential community to the south.

"The solidity of a Chicago cop. The squat comfort of a bungalow. Christmas decorations on taverns. The way I shudder when the El passes overhead. The beauty of Latino kids in Little Village. The cleaning-lady madonnas in the Loop. The altar-boy sound of bells ringing on a Mexican popsicle vendor's cart. How people talk. Cabbies who wave to you when you let them 'cut in.' Below-street-level-gardens in Pilsen. The steam table democracy of Manny's Deli. Smoke from summertime barbecues in empty lots.
I love it here!"
—Phil Ponce, televison news host

Above: Though Chicago's most elegant residential districts originally spread south, until recently these areas have not been as widely recognized as their north-side counterparts. Today the richness and variety of the south side's architecture and culture are being rediscovered. An example is the Oakland neighborhood's modest but delightful Berkeley Cottages (a dozen in all), built in 1887. Unfortunately, a now-abandoned public housing project cuts off access from these charming homes to the lakeshore to the east.

Right top: Focal point of the 1893 World's Columbian Exposition was Daniel Chester French's Statue of the Republic. *A scaled-down replica still graces Jackson Park, south of the Museum of Science and Industry, where the fair was held.*

Right: In the mid-1880s, industrialist George S. Pullman decided to site the new manufacturing plant for his Palace Car Company near Lake Calumet on the city's far south side. Thinking his workers would be healthier (and thus more productive) if they lived in wholesome surroundings, he enlisted architect S. S. Beman to devise a planned community for his employees. As with other paternalistic, utopian notions, this one did not work well in practice, but Beman's lovely neighborhood still stands much unchanged. Sunday brunch at the community's Hotel Florence (pictured here) is a popular weekend treat.

"Chicago is a big city with small town attitudes of friendliness, helpfulness, and 'I can get the job done no matter how big it is or how hard I have to work.' It is America."
—John E. Ruhaak, airline executive

Above: Chicago's boulevard system is an often-overlooked city asset. For example, Drexel Boulevard, running through Kenwood on the south side, was planned by the firm of Olmsted and Vaux, famed for their design of New York's Central Park. Many elegant mansions still line the graceful boulevard. This one was built in 1887 for lumber fortune heir Martin A. Ryerson, who would later win fame for his foresighted acquisitions for the Art Institute's collections.

Left: Originally designed in 1890 by famed architects Dankmar Adler and Louis Sullivan to serve a Jewish congregation, this extraordinary structure now serves as the Pilgrim Baptist Church. Its choir leader, Thomas A. Dorsey, brought additional renown to the building in the 1930s when he convinced church fathers that gospel music was indeed an appropriate way to worship. The rest is history.

Above: The 1836 Widow Clarke House, the city's oldest remaining structure, is part of the Prairie Avenue Historic District on 18th Street just east of Michigan Avenue. Once the city's most elegant community—home to the Fields, Pullmans, Armours, and other leading families—the area today only hints of its grand past. Some of the history lingers, however, including the Widow Clarke House and the innovative, fortresslike 1887 Glessner House. Both historic homes are open to the public daily for tours.

Left: A Sunday afternoon study group welcomes two young members in the Austin neighborhood's Greater Love Missionary Baptist Church.

Opposite top: Pilsen, on the lower west side, has long been a port of entry for immigrants ranging from the early Czechs to present-day Mexicans, who call it Pueblo Pequeño or Little Village. Their heritage is celebrated with events like the Via Crucis (the Way of the Cross reenactment the week before Easter) and a lively summertime Fiesta del Sol.

Opposite bottom: Chicago's Chinatown covers several city blocks just two El stops south of the Loop. **Left:** This detail from the neighborhood's On Leong Building is emblematic of surrounding restaurants and shops, which deal in everything from Peking duck to porcelain vases. **Right:** Neighborhood friends enjoy a summer day on a Ferris wheel in Chinatown.

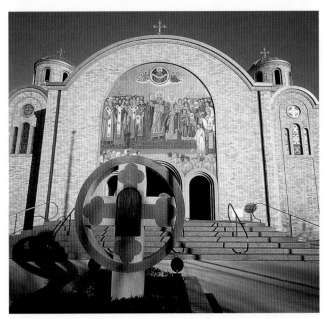

Above left: In the nineteenth century, before U.S. cities began establishing extensive park systems, graciously designed cemeteries were preferred places for Sunday strolls. Chicago's north-side Graceland and south-side Oak Woods are both prime examples of this era. Oak Woods doesn't boast as many well-known gravesites as Graceland, but one that is visited regularly is that of Mayor Harold Washington, who is buried near this tree glimmering in the late-fall light of a setting sun.

Above right: Graceland headstones constitute a who's who of Chicago's past. Many of the monuments are far more grand than that of architect Louis Sullivan, though his eloquently reflects his use of organically inspired decoration and his dictum that form follows function.

Left: The mosaic dominating the entrance to Saints Volodymyr and Olha Church in Ukrainian Village commemorates the conversion to Christianity of the Grand Duke Vladimir of Kiev in 988.

Opposite: The Holy Trinity Russian Orthodox Cathedral combines Byzantine and Orthodox elements in an area west of downtown. In 1889, immigrants commissioned Louis Sullivan to create a building that would resemble provincial churches in their homeland.

"I urge people to take a very special look at Chicago, to see the people and their neighborhoods, to discover the contributions made by all the various ethnic groups through their folk arts, shops, religious ornamentation, architecture, and customs, retained to the present day. Beyond the thrilling architecture, beautiful parks, fabulous shopping, and delicious eating opportunities, the city is an unending mosaic of ethnic variety. 'In Chicago, you can get a job,' the immigrants heard and heeded the call. We're all in their debt."
—Leah Joy Axelrod, tour company owner

Above: Prototypical Chicago, one might say of this street in Edgewater, on the north side. On a hazy, lazy Fourth of July, flowers bloom, bushes are clipped, and flags fly. Named because of its proximity to Lake Michigan, the neighborhood is equally attractive because of its good and affordable housing and the numerous El stops in the community.

Right, both photos: Devon Avenue on Chicago's northwest side offers the city's liveliest ethnic melange. Part of it is called Golda Meir Way to honor its Russian and Jewish residents. Farther east, it is Gandhi Marg for the Indian merchants and families there, including the young group in this portrait. Recently, Koreans have begun to call Devon Avenue home, too.

Above: Gracious high- and mid-rise residences ring Lincoln Park's lagoons, zoo, and charming Cafe Brauer, a gathering place and restaurant shown here in the middle of the park.

Left: Austin, on Chicago's far west side, provides another fascinating glimpse at Chicago history. A staunchly independent town until it was annexed by the city in 1899, it retains much of its distinctiveness. A family dog greets visitors to the 1887 Catherine Schlecht House, a late-Victorian structure that is being lovingly restored.

"What makes the city unique is that for all of its cosmopolitan advantages Chicago is still the biggest small town in America. It's still a city of neighborhoods, in which people know their wards and ward heelers, parishes and precinct captains; a city that's retained its sense of community. Chicago is still a city people proudly call their home."
—David Axelrod, political consultant

89

Above: This landmarked street called Alta Vista Terrace near Wrigley Field is noted for the human scale and distinctive harmony of the houses here.

Right: Beginning in the 1850s, street and sidewalk levels were raised to make way for an underground sanitation system. These homes in Wicker Park near Division and Ashland typify this distinction of Chicago's domestic design.

Right bottom: Successive waves of German and Swedish residents settled Lake View on the north side, an independent town until 1889. One of the area's major industries was brickmaking—hence, its fanciful use on some neighborhood buildings.

"The wonderment that I find in Chicago is its diversity. You can drive from one neighborhood to another and it's like you have traveled out of town; the neighborhood characteristics are so different. A mere car ride can take you from Chinatown to Little Italy; from Pilsen with its Bohemian past and Mexican present to the black communities of South Shore and Chatham; to tony Lincoln Park to beautiful Beverly and historic Pullman—all this and you've never left town. This diversity is our richness, but it's also our problem. Some people view the ethnic differences as a clash, but I see them as a beautiful gumbo blend."
—Hermene Hartman, newspaper publisher

Winter comes gracefully to Lincoln Park's Farm-in-the-Zoo. The chill leaves these ducks a lagoon to themselves and seemingly little to eat. But not to worry: feeding them is a very popular pastime.

Index

For More Information

Chicago Architecture Foundation. 224 South Michigan Avenue, Chicago, IL 60604-2507. 312-922-3432. **Information available:** Offers tours of the downtown area and neighborhoods via foot, bus, and boat, plus a regular series of lectures. Schedules are available by phone or mail. Its headquarters include a giftshop and exhibits.

Chicago Convention and Tourism Bureau. 2301 South Lake Shore Drive, Chicago, IL 60616. 312-567-8500. **Information available:** Provides material on conventions automatically via fax machine. Also publishes *Chicago Guidebook* available through state and city tourism offices.

Chicago Office of Tourism. Chicago Cultural Center, 78 East Washington, Chicago, IL 60602. 312-744-2400 or 800-487-2446. **Information available:** *Visitors' Map and Guide* and quarterly *Calendar of Events.*

Chicagoland Chamber of Commerce. One IBM Plaza, Suite 2800, Chicago, IL 60611. 312-744-2400. **Information available:** Provides relocation packages for businesses and individuals, plus a variety of services for the area business community.

Illinois Bureau of Tourism. James R. Thompson Center, 100 West Randolph St., 3-400, Chicago, IL 60601. 800-223-0121 (9 A.M. to 11 P.M.). **Information available:** *Illinois Visitor's Guide,* state map, phone numbers for accommodations.

Performance Hotlines. Several art organizations provide 24-hour hotlines with recorded information on a variety of performances. For dance, call 312-419-8383; for popular music, call 312-666-6667; for classical music, call 312-987-9296; for jazz, call 312-427-3000. The Chicago Fine Arts Hotline at 312-346-3278 provides information on free performances in the Chicago Cultural Center and under the Picasso sculpture on Daley Plaza.

Special Events Hotline. Mayor's Office of Special Events. 312-744-3370. **Information available:** A frequently updated 24-hour hotline providing information about happenings in town.

VISITOR INFORMATION CENTERS. The main center is in the Historic Water Tower, but there are visitor booths at the other locations listed below. They provide city maps and guidebooks, information on events and attractions, museum exhibitions and performances, and accommodations. Each is staffed by personnel happy to answer additional questions.

Chicago's Historic Water Tower. 806 North Michigan Avenue, Chicago, IL 60611 (at Chicago Avenue).

Chicago Cultural Center. 77 East Randolph Street, Chicago, IL 60601 (at Michigan Avenue).

O'Hare International Airport. Baggage Levels, Terminals 1 and 2.

Midway Airport. 5800 South Cicero Avenue, Chicago, IL 60638.

Suggested Readings

Cronon, William. *Nature's Metropolis: Chicago and the Great West.* New York: W.W. Norton, 1991.

Danilov, Viktor J. *Chicago's Museums: A Complete Guide to the City's Cultural Attractions.* Chicago: Chicago Review Press, 1991.

Hayner, Don, and Tom McNamee. *Metro Chicago Almanac.* Chicago: Bonus books and Chicago Sun-Times, 1991.

Hayner, Don, and Tom McNamee. *Streetwise Chicago: A History of Chicago Street Names.* Chicago: Loyola University Press, 1988.

Heise, Kenan. *The Chicagoization of America, 1893–1917.* Evanston, IL: Chicago Historical Bookworks, 1990.

Lindberg, Richard C. *Ethnic Chicago: A Complete Guide to the Many Faces & Cultures of Chicago.* Lincolnwood, IL: Passport Books, 1993.

Mayer, Harold M., and Richard C. Wade. *Chicago: Growth of a Metropolis.* Chicago: University of Chicago Press, 1969.

Pacyga, Dominic A., and Ellen Skerrett. *Chicago: City of Neighborhoods.* Chicago: Loyola University Press, 1986.

Sawyers, June Skinner. *Chicago Portraits: Biographies of 250 Famous Chicagoans.* Chicago: Loyola University Press, 1991.

Sinkevitch, Alice, and AIA (American Institue of Architects). *Guide to Chicago.* San Diego: Harcourt Brace, 1993.

About the
Author and Photographer

Photo © by Christopher J. Berrafato

Marilyn D. Clancy was born in Chicago and has lived either in the city or the adjacent suburb of Oak Park all of her life. She is the president of Clancy & Company, a communications, management, and marketing firm. "D.," as her friends know her, is the founding executive director of the Chicago Tourism Council. She has been extremely active in community groups involved in many fields, including tourism, politics, and the arts. D. is married to William Clancy, and they have four children.

Ron Schramm, a native of the south side of Chicago, now makes his home on the north side of the city. After a tour of infantry duty in Vietnam, he received his Bachelor's of Arts in 1975 from Columbia College. In 1979 he began to photograph the city for promotional clients and has built an extensive file of Chicago subjects. His work has been published widely in a variety of media. He is married to Ann Schramm and has two children, Zachary and Ellen.